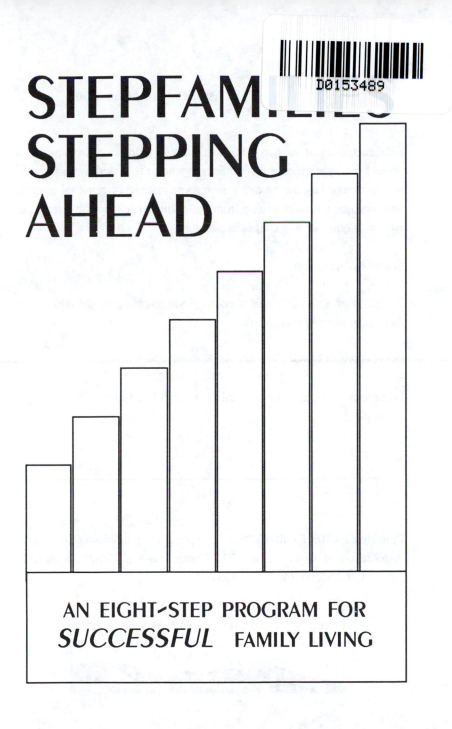

STEPFAMILIES STEPPING AHEAD

AN EIGHT-STEP PROGRAM FOR *SUCCESSFUL* FAMILY LIVING

Edited by Mala Burt

Third edition. Originally published in 1988 as *Stepping Ahead: A Program for Successful Stepfamily Living.*

ISBN 0-9624432-0-4

Library of Congress Catalog Card Number: 89-051436

Published by STEPFAMILIES PRESS, the publishing division of Stepfamily Association of America, Inc., 215 Centennial Mall South, Suite 212, Lincoln, NE 68508. (402) 477-7837

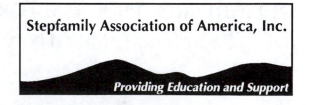

Stepfamily Association of America, Inc.

Providing Education and Support

Table of Contents

Foreword

I am exceedingly honored to have been asked to write the foreword for this, the fourth printing of *Stepfamilies Stepping Ahead: An Eight Step Program for Successful Stepfamily Living*. As a therapist working mostly with stepfamily couples or individuals who are in, or about to enter stepfamilies, I am in daily contact with the pain, frustration, and confusion most couples or families experience as they begin to traverse the complex road to stepfamily integration. But this slim information-packed volume, first published in 1988, offers a beacon of light and direction, leading individuals forward into a family of satisfying relationships.

Stepfamilies Stepping Ahead was written by two past presidents of SAA with the collaboration of clinicians, researchers, and stepfamily members from across the United States.

The book is a progressive step by step guide which begins by defining a stepfamily, then moves on to clarify common but inaccurate beliefs about stepfamilies. Moving ahead, the reader begins to understand stepfamilies, the importance of knowing how and why stepfamilies are different from intact families, and the tasks that will lead to stepfamily integration. Finally *Stepfamilies Stepping Ahead* closes with the Stepping Ahead Program for successful stepfamily living. I recommend this book to all of my clients, support group members, and anyone even remotely considering the stepfamily experience. I heartily recommend it to you.

As a longstanding member of SAA and its current President, I wish you good reading and great joy in your own personal stepfamily journey.

—Judith L. Bauersfeld, Ph.D.
President SAA 1991-1993.

WHAT IS A STEPFAMILY?

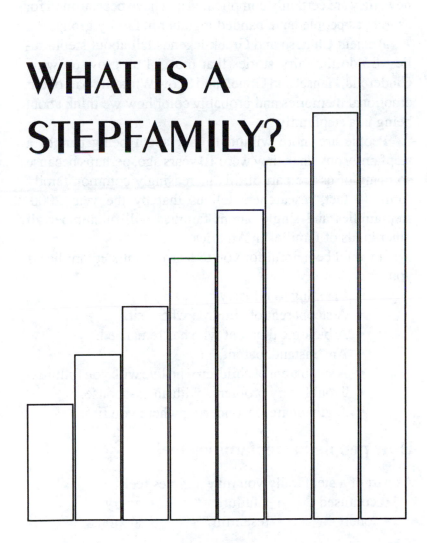

What is a stepfamily?

You are in a stepfamily if you or your partner has children from a previous relationship. Although stepfamilies are not new, they are certainly complicated and have been around for as long as people have banded together in family groups.

Ancient Chinese and Greek legends tell about stepfamilies. So do the fairy stories that most of us grow up with. Cinderella, Hansel and Gretel, and Snow White are part of our emotional memories and probably color how we think about being in a stepfamily.

People are more willing to talk about being part of a stepfamily now than they were 10 years ago, perhaps because so many of us are part of this increasingly common family form. In fact, researchers tell us that by the year 2000, stepfamilies and single-parent families will outnumber all other kinds of families in America.

It would be helpful for you to learn about stepfamilies if you are:

- Planning to remarry.
- A stepparent of children who visit.
- A biological parent who has remarried.
- An "instant" parent.
- A stepparent of children who live with you fulltime.
- Troubled by problems with an ex-spouse.
- A grandparent wondering where you fit in.

How people in stepfamilies feel.

As part of a stepfamily you may at times feel:

- confused
- a failure
- angry
- lonely
- resentful
- anxious

- overwhelmed
- insecure
- hopeful
- wicked
- cheated
- rejected by stepchildren
- isolated
- despairing

These feelings are common. They are uncomfortable because you have high hopes for your new marriage. Often, you may be afraid that things won't work out. Lots of people don't talk about being part of a stepfamily. Sometimes people don't even identify that that is the situation for them. You may think you are the only one who has ever felt this way. There are lots of people in your situation (people who want their family life to be more satisfying and who sometimes also feel frustrated, angry, hurt and hopeful).

People in stepfamilies may feel frustrated when:

- They suddenly have people react to them as though they are a wicked stepparent.
- Their lives are frequently disrupted by situations over which they have no control.
- They don't seem to have any influence in the household.
- They feel like intruders and outsiders.
- They feel pushed to love stepchildren.
- They have never been parents before and everyone assumes they know how to parent.
- They have no privacy.
- They and their partners don't agree on discipline.
- They are biological parents feeling caught in the middle between their children and their new spouses.

People in stepfamilies may feel angry when:

- They support somebody else's child.
- Their partner doesn't seem to want to let them be part of the family.

- Children's needs always seem to take priority.
- This new marriage doesn't live up to their fantasy.
- They feel they are giving up more than they are getting.
- Plans for a new life take a back seat because of previous financial commitments made by their partner.
- Visitation seems to be at the whim of the custodial parent.

People in stepfamilies may feel hurt when:
- They are rejected by stepchildren.
- They feel abandoned by their spouse.
- They are not given any status in the new family.
- Their efforts are not appreciated.
- They want to have a child and their partner is "parented out."

People in stepfamilies feel hopeful when:
- They feel more in control.
- They have more knowledge about how stepfamilies work and the stages of stepfamily development.
- They can see a relationship with a stepchild beginning to bud.
- They find group support such as an SAA Chapter.

Some things can change. Some things can't. You can learn to tell the difference and put your energy where it will count. You can learn to reevaluate your expectations (and perhaps lower them). You can learn to make small steps toward the goal of having this new family feel like a comfortable, nurturing place to live.

THE MYTHS ABOUT STEPFAMILIES

The myths about stepfamilies

Myths are beliefs that strongly influence the way people in stepfamilies adjust to their new family and react to one another. The following myths about stepfamilies can be stumbling blocks on the stepfamily journey.

Myth #1. Love occurs instantly between the child and the stepparent.

This is the expectation that because you love your new partner you will automatically love his or her children. Or that the children will automatically love us because we are such nice people. Of course, if we think about it, we recognize that establishing relationships takes time, that it does not happen overnight or by magic.

Even if we recognize the time factor involved, it is hard to accept that sometimes we are willing to have a relationship with someone who is not willing to have a relationship with us. That hurts, and when people hurt, they may become resentful and angry.

Stepfamily adjustment will be helped if we come to the relationships with our stepchildren with minimal, and, therefore, more realistic, expectations about how the relationships will develop. We may then be pleased when respect and friendship blossom and less disappointed if it takes more time than we anticipated.

Myth #2. Children of divorce and remarriage are forever damaged.

Children go through a painful period of adjustment after a divorce or remarriage. Adults often respond to their children's pain with guilt. Somehow they feel they can "make it up" to them. This leads to difficulties in responding appropriately to our children's hurt and setting appropriate limits — an important part of parenting.

Researchers have hopeful news about children of divorce and remarriage. Although it takes some time, most children do recover their emotional equilibrium. Five and 10 years later most are found to be no different, in many important ways, from kids in first marriage families.

Myth #3 Stepmothers are wicked.

This myth is based on the fairy stories we all hear as children. Because these stories tell about stepmothers who are not kind, nice or fair, we may be confused about our roles when we become stepmothers. We are nice people, wanting to do a good job, but the world seems to have another idea about stepmothers.

This negative concept of the stepmother role impacts us in a very personal way and we may be very self-conscious about our stepparenting. Research tells us that stepmothers have the most difficult role in the stepfamily. (But, if you are a stepmother, you knew that already!)

Myth #4 *Adjustment to stepfamily life occurs quickly.*

People are optimistic and hopeful when they remarry. They want life to settle down and to get on with being happy. If your hope or expectation is that once the wedding vows are spoken life will return to normal (whatever that is), you are going to be disappointed.

Because stepfamilies are such complicated families, the time it takes for people to get to know each other, to create positive relationships, and to develop some family history is significant, usually at least four years.

Myth #5 *Children adjust to divorce and remarriage more easily if biological fathers (or mothers) withdraw.*

Children will always have two biological parents and will adjust better if they have access to both. This means they need to be able to see their nonresidential parent and to think well of him (or her). Sometimes visitation is painful for the nonresidential parent, but it is very important to the child's adjustment and emotional health, except in those rare instances of parental abuse or neglect.

It is helpful if the residential parent and stepparent can work toward a "parenting partnership" with all the adults involved. Sometimes this can't happen right away, but it can be something to work toward.

Myth #6 *Stepfamilies formed after a parent dies are easier.*

People need time to grieve the loss of a loved one, and a remarriage may "reactivate" unfinished grieving. These emotional issues may get played out in the new relationship with detrimental effects.

Another problem is that it can be difficult to think realistically about the person who has died. He or she exists in memory, not in reality, and sometimes gets elevated to sainthood.

When people remarry after the death of a spouse, they may want a relationship similar to the one before. When people remarry after a divorce, they are usually looking for something very different. New partners may find themselves competing with a ghost.

Myth #7 Part-time stepfamilies are easier.

Relationships take time; or stepfamilies where the children visit only occasionally are hampered by the lack of time to work on relationships.

If your stepchildren come every other weekend, there is less time for one-on-one time between the stepchild and stepparent and less time for family activities. Since stepfamilies follow a process of transition (stages of development), it may take the part-time stepfamily longer to move through the process.

Myth #8 There is only one kind of family.

This is the myth that says you will be just like a first marriage (or biological) family. Today there are lots of different kinds of families; first marriage, single parent and stepfamilies to name a few. Each is valuable and has different characteristics. Just because there are two adults in the stepfamily doesn't mean that it recreates a biological family. If this is what you are hoping for, you will be frustrated when it doesn't happen.

HOW STEPFAMILIES ARE DIFFERENT

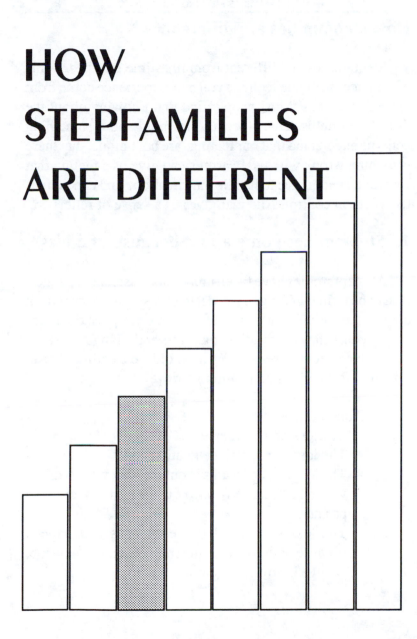

How stepfamilies are different.

Stepfamilies are different from first-time families. Some of the uncomfortable feelings you may experience come from these differences. Most people find that knowing about the differences helps. That's because learning about something helps us understand that our feelings are not unique, that there is nothing wrong with us. Learning can give us a feeling that we will be better able to handle our situation, and can help us feel more in control. And that gives us a sense of relief!

1. Stepfamilies come about because of a loss.

All stepfamilies have faced numerous losses and changes. It may be a final ending... the death of a spouse or parent. It may be the ending of a marriage or relationship. Endings are hard because they mean adjusting to loss and change. Because people have trouble separating from old ties, endings mean grieving. Both adults and children grieve.

Adults grieve:
- The loss of a partner.
- The loss of a marriage relationship.
- The loss of our dreams about the way we thought it would be because we are not "the first" for our new partner.
- The losses involved in the changes that happen because of the death or divorce (moving, a new job, change in life style, etc.).

Children grieve:
- The loss of a parent (even if the nonresidential parent visits regularly).
- The loss or lessened availability of the remaining parent when courtship and remarriage occur.
- The loss of stability.
- The changes that happen because of the divorce or death (new place to live, new school, loss of friends etc.).
- The loss of their fantasy of family the way they want it to be.

Unresolved grief can sometimes be seen in the continued warfare and hostility between some parents, or in the inability of a child to accept a stepparent. Children and adults may still be grieving when remarriage takes place, or the grieving may be "reactivated" at that time.

2. The parent/child relationship has a longer history than the new couple's relationship.

This can make it difficult for the adults to feel as though they are the primary, long-term relationship. It also means that the incoming marriage partner often feels like an intruder or outsider. Sometimes the close relationships that develop between parents and children in single parent households mean that the new adult partner has difficulty "being allowed in." Even the parent who looks forward to having someone share the load may find it hard to let a new partner help with parenting duties.

All of us have emotional "memory books." When parents

and their children get together and "remember," it is like turning the pages of the book they made together. The difficulty for the stepparent is that he or she is not in this memory book, but his or her partner's "ex" **is**. Stepparents need to be aware that creating a stepfamily memory book takes time and can only be accomplished as people share activities.

The memory book you create with your partner is also vitally important. It means that when life gets difficult, you will be able to leaf through your book and remember the good times, the funny stories, the romantic interludes, even the difficult times you have overcome. It takes time to build a history with your partner, and the memories created with your spouse don't have to compete with the memories they have with their children. But, it does help you understand why sometimes stepparents feel on the outside.

3. A biological parent (ex-spouse) is in another place.

Even if the other parent never visits or has died, he or she is a part of the children's past (just as you have people in your past whom your partner and stepchildren and children don't know). Children need to be allowed to have memories of their other parent. They need to be allowed to have pictures and to talk about the other parent. If a stepparent can't tolerate this very well, the biological parent can help out here by allowing the child time to recall past experiences. Research tells us that the children who adjust the best to divorce are those who have the easiest access to both their parents. This means they can talk to , write and/or see their nonresidential parent as often as possible.

It is important that a child be given permission (by the parent and stepparent) to love the other biological parent. It is also important for the child to be given permission by both biological parents to like the stepparent(s). Children who are asked to choose are put in a no-win emotional dilemma. **Remember:** to accept the present we need to accept and allow for one another's past.

4. Children are members of two households.

"Where do I belong?" and "Where do I fit in?" are questions asked by many stepchildren. Children have the ability to adjust to two sets of rules or two ways of doing things as long as they are not asked to choose which is better.

It is important for parent and stepparent to talk about rules for the household, rules for behavior of the children and the consequences for broken rules. Once the adults are clear about the rules, they need to be communicated to the children in the family by the biological parent.

Authorities recommend that at the beginning, discipline come from the biological parent. This means that parent and stepparent decide on the rules together but that the biological parent announces the rules and enforces the consequences. Later, after relationships have developed, the stepparent can become more involved. Adults also need to understand that there is a difference between "parenting" and "discipline." Parenting has to do with things such as nurturing ("I love you."), transmitting values ("It's important to do the best you can."), giving positive strokes ("You really did a good job."), maintaining appropriate boundaries in the family ("Your mother and I are talking now about a grown up decision."), and setting appropriate limits on children's behavior ("You can play after the dishes are done."). Discipline has to do with enforcing consequences when values, boundaries and limits are not observed.

Flexibility on the part of the adults in one household can help to establish a "parenting partnership" with the other household. If this can happen, adults and children benefit. Often this parenting partnership cannot be established until feelings about the divorce and remarriage have settled down, but it is a goal worth working for.

5. Stepparents may be asked to assume a parental role before emotional ties with the stepchild have been established.

Often a stepparent is thrust into the role of "instant parent." With no previous parenting experience, this person is asked to play a knowledgeable parent role in the household. Biological parents grow into their parenting roles as their children grow. Stepparents are often expected to adjust instantly as though parenting is an inborn skill. It is not!!!

For biological parents, the bonding process that happens means we are more tolerant of our children's personalities and behaviors than someone who doesn't know them so well. This is normal. The reverse is also true. Children are bonded to (and thus often more tolerant of) their biological parents.

Parents can assist the stepparent by helping them to "get to know" their child. They can show them the picture albums, run the home movies, tell the family stories and help fill in the gaps. Some children will enjoy being a part of this process. The painful part for the stepparent may be the presence in the history of the child's other biological parent. Be aware that your acceptance of this parent will help this child be less resistant to you. You can be reassuring to the child that while you have an adult role in this household, you will not try to replace his or her other parent. Many stepparents find a satisfactory role in simply being a "helper" to the biological parent. This can work well, especially where stepchildren are elementary school age or older.

6. There is no legal relationship between stepparents and stepchildren.

This lack of a legal relationship (we are not birth, adoptive, or foster parents) is another reason our role as stepparent is unclear. There is a loss of status which may give us a feeling of wanting to be less involved. Yet there may be a sense of having legal responsibility — responsibility without authority.

No legal relationship with our stepchild means that, unless we have written authority, we can't authorize emergency medical care, have access to school records or sign important documents. You may want to have written authority if you care for minor stepchildren. This can be secured by being granted a limited power of attorney (for example, to authorize emergency medical care) by the biological parent.

This form, **which should be notarized by a notary public to be effective,** can read as follows:

I, _____
(Name of biological /custodial parent.)

_____of
(Indicate whether father/mother of child(ren).)

_____
(Names(s) of child(ren).)

whose birthday(s) is/are: _____,
(Fill in birthday(s).)

hereby allow_____
(Name of stepparent/caretaker of child(ren).)

to secure medical attention/treatment/tests on behalf of my
child(ren).

_____
(Signature of biological/custodial parent.) *

*This limited power of attorney was prepared by Richard Victor, Esq., a
member of STEPFAMILY ASSOCIATION OF AMERICA, INC.
FORM MAY BE REPRODUCED.

Legal issues which create stress for stepfamilies can
involve inheritance, last names, and potential visitation issues
if this new family should end because of death or divorce.
Fortunately, the laws are beginning to change, but it's taking
them a long time to catch up.

These six ways in which stepfamilies are different mean
that you have some tasks to accomplish when you form a
stepfamily. These will take some time. As you work on these
tasks together, you will be moving towards the variety of
rewarding experiences and relationships that being part of a
stepfamily can bring.

TASKS FOR STEPFAMILIES

Guidelines for Accomplishing Stepfamily Tasks

The "bottom-line" task for stepfamilies is to establish a new family identity. There are a number of tasks (based on the differences between first marriage families and stepfamilies) that need to be accomplished in order to do this. Some strategies for helping to accomplish each task are suggested. Some tasks are more difficult and you may not be able to accomplish them all right away. The "Stepping Ahead" program at the end of this book will help you.

1. Task: dealing with losses and changes.

It helps to remember that each person in the family experiences loss since all change involves letting go of former situations and relationships. Children usually would prefer to remain in their previous family pattern and often get angry and act in annoying ways, rather than crying and feeling sad. Reading books, introducing changes slowly, and helping them to talk about their sadness can make it more possible for adults and children to say goodbye to the past and begin to appreciate the gains of the new family unit.

> Strategies:
> * Identify/recognize losses for all individuals.
> * Support expressions of sadness.
> * Help children talk about, instead of acting out feelings.
> * Read stepfamily books.Many books for children are available.
> * Make changes gradually.
> * See that everyone gets a turn.

- Inform children of plans involving them.
- Accept the insecurity of change.

2. Task: Negotiate different developmental needs.

In a remarriage, adults and children are at different places in their lives. One partner may have been married before and the other may have been unmarried; one may have been a parent, and the other partner may not have children; both may have children but be unfamiliar with or have forgotten what children of certain ages are like; children may be adolescents who have reached an age where they would rather be with their friends than become involved in forming a new family unit. These differences usually mean that some of the needs of the individuals will not fit together easily. As a result, it may take a lot of flexibility and tolerance and talking about these differences to find the best ways of satisfying as many of these needs as possible.

Strategies:
- Take a child development and/or parenting class.
- Accept validity of different life cycle phases for adults and children.
- Communicate individual needs clearly.
- Negotiate incompatible needs.
- Develop tolerance and flexibility.

3. Task: establishing new traditions.

Children and adults have been used to eating certain foods,

following certain patterns of activity and doing a million things in very different ways. Many times you aren't even aware of how you do something until someone else does the same thing in a different way. It's hard not to feel that your way is **right** and that the other way is **wrong**! Instead, compare notes about the ways that all household members have celebrated holidays and birthdays, what kinds of foods they like, and how everyday events have been handled.

How does everyone want things to go in your present household? Combine former ways of doing things (perhaps turkey and ham for Thanksgiving). Take turns with others (a family drive one Sunday, playing Monopoly the next), and start new traditions that will become special for your new family.

The couple and, whenever possible, the children, too, need to decide together on the house rules, but stepparents need to form a friendly relationship with their stepchildren before attempting to see that the house rules are followed. The parent of the children needs to set the limits at the beginning.

Strategies:
- Recognize ways are different, not right or wrong.
- Concentrate on important situations only.
- Stepparents take on discipline enforcement slowly.
- Use "family meetings" for problem solving and giving appreciation.
- Shift "givens" slowly whenever possible.
- Retain/combine appropriate rituals.
- Enrich with new creative traditions.

4. Task: developing a solid couple bond.

It is easy for adults to spend so much time and energy doing their best to make the household run smoothly that they forget to take care of their own needs for fun and relaxation as a couple. It usually takes active planning ahead for the adults to make time for themselves. Developing and enjoying yourselves as a couple is important not only for you but also for the children, although they may resent it at first. This is because children need to have a strong couple to give them family stability and to teach them how to work together as a couple when they mature, leave home, and form their own couple relationships.

> Strategies:
> - Accept the couple relationship as primary and long-term.
> - Nourish couple relationship.
> - Plan for couple "alone time."
> - Decide general household rules as a couple.
> - Support one another regarding the children.
> - Expect and accept different parent/stepparent-child feelings.
> - Work out money matters together.

5. Task: forming new relationships.

Creating bonds between individuals generally takes considerable time because good relationships are the result of sharing many happy and satisfying times together. Learning about one another and doing things in pairs can help this process. It may be hard for a parent to step back a little so that the stepparent and stepchildren have a chance to be together, but this is one of the best ways to work toward building new relationships. This helps the people in the household to begin to feel like a family group. At times, particularly with older children, strong bonds of caring may not develop. However, a stepparent can be "fair" to stepchildren even when they have not developed a warm relationship.

Strategies:
- Fill in past histories.
- Make stepparent-stepchild one-on-one time.
- Make parent-child one-on-one time.
- Parent make space for stepparent-stepchild relationship.
- Do not expect "instant love" and adjustment.
- Be fair to stepchildren even when caring has not developed.
- Follow children's lead in what to call stepparent.
- Do fun things together.

6. Task: creating a "parent coalition."

Developing a civil relationship among the adults who are involved in raising the children benefits everyone even though there may be very little contact among the adults. Having a neutral businesslike relationship can reduce the adult's fears of the children's acceptance of both parents and stepparents. Former marriage relationships have ended, but parent/child relationships continue. Even if these contacts do not occur very often, they can help children feel more loved and increase their self esteem.

Strategies:
- Deal directly with parenting adults in other households.
- Parents keep children out of the middle.
- Do not talk negatively about parent in other household.
- Control what you can and accept limitations.
- Avoid power struggles between households.
- Respect parenting skills of former spouse.
- Contribute own "specialness" to children.
- Communicate between households in most effective manner.

7. Task: accepting continual shifts in household composition.

Getting used to the comings and goings of children can take some time. After a while such changes can feel "normal." Don't save all special events for times when nonresident children are present. If you do, the "resident" children may feel that the "nonresident" children are more loved and special. While these changes can upset the routine of the household they also mean that the adults have a rest from their parenting responsibilities.

Strategies:
- Allow children to enjoy their households.
- Give children time to adjust to household switches.
- Avoid asking children to be "messengers" or "spies."
- Consider a teenager's serious desire to change residence.

- Respect privacy (boundaries) of all households.
- Set consequences that affect only your own household.
- Provide personal place for nonresident children.
- Plan special times for various household constellations.

8. Task: risking involvement despite little support from society.

Even though they may not have a legal status, stepparent/stepchild relationships can be very rewarding. Children gain by having more adults to care about them, and stepparents gain from the satisfaction of contributions to the children's lives. Even when a stepfamily is disrupted by divorce or the death of a parent, it can be important for stepparents to be active in maintaining these relationships.

Strategies:
- Include stepparents in school, religious, sports activities, etc.
- Give legal permission for stepparent to act when necessary.
- Continue stepparent-stepchild relationships, after death or divorce, when bonds have developed.
- Stepparent include self in stepchild's activities.
- Find groups supportive of stepfamilies.
- Remember that all relationships involve risk.*

* Reprinted from the *Stepfamily Workshop Manual* by permission of the authors, Emily Visher, Ph.D., and John Visher, M.D.

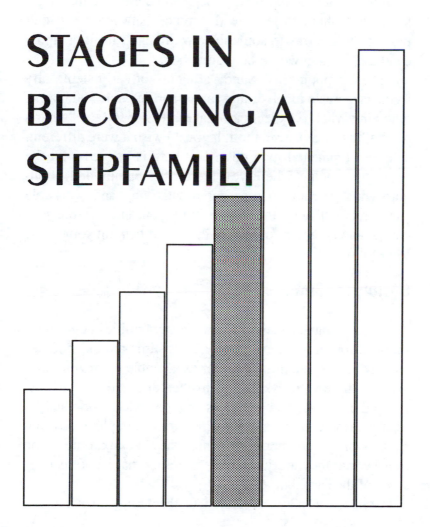

STAGES IN
BECOMING A
STEPFAMILY

Seven steps to becoming a new family

Stepfamily living requires traversing a geography that has some similarities and many differences from biological family living. The terrain is often rocky and confusing making it particularly hard to tell the difference between a difficult passage on the way to someplace warm and fulfilling and a dead end. A map would be a great help.

The disappointments and "glitches" of early stepfamily living can create much of that same snarl of panic and blame. Knowing what to expect can make it easier to face "what's normal" as a team, even though you all wish it were different. The developmental map described here is offered with the hope that finding where you are on the bumpy and often-harrowing journey to creating a satisfying and workable stepfamily will make the trip easier for you, and will free your energy and attention for the challenges of making your home life satisfying.

Biological families

First we have to talk about how stepfamilies begin their journey forming a new family. First-time-around couples usually have some time together as a couple before children arrive — time to get to know each other, time to figure out how to handle the fact that she likes spicy Mexican food and he likes meat and potatoes. First-time-around couples also often have a honeymoon period in which they can luxuriate in the fantasy that they are just alike, a feeling that smooths over some of the early bumps.

Children usually are added to the family one by one,

allowing the couple to slowly evolve parenting roles, establish rhythms, develop shared values, and build family rituals.

Divorce or death ushers in an era of single-parent family living. Most children of divorce become part of two single-parent families, with living arrangements as varied as the families that create them. In this period, children must adjust to not only having only one parent at a time, but to moving between two very different households, and often moving to a new community.

During this time, the single-parent and child(ren) often turn to each other for activities that would have been shared with another adult — planning time and money, sharing evenings by the television, cuddling in the morning. Discipline in single-parent families tends to be more lax — it is hard enough to hold the line with two parents, and very hard with only one parent, who is often exhausted and who has no one else to turn to for support when children don't welcome limits. The "exceptional closeness" which often develops between child and parent is a normal part of single-parent family living.

Stepfamily beginnings: It's no honeymoon.

The stepfamily begins, then, with the stepparent cast as an outsider in a strong parent-child "mini-family." This biological mini-family has a shared history, shared rules, shared rituals and shared understanding of what's OK to do with wet bath towels, where the silverware goes on the table, and how holidays are celebrated. These rules have built up over the years and intensified in the single-parent family.

This family structure and history make for a very different start for stepfamilies. Adults not only have no honeymoon period, but they begin the gargantuan task of parenting before they even have time to get to know each other. They are also faced immediately and squarely with the painful experience of feeling fundamentally different about the children they must parent together: The biological parent feels pulled, engaged, worried, protective and eager to please. The stepparent often feels rejected, ignored and competitive with the same child.

All of this means the biological parent and the children begin with the strongest relationship, not the parents. Family therapists have said over and over that families function best when the adult couple is the strongest unit, is able to work as a team to make decisions and provide enough nourishment, protection, and direction for all members of the family. The stepfamily's task is to move from a biological mini-family with a stepparent outsider (or when both adults bring kids, to move from two warring mini-families) to a family unified by a strong cooperative couple. This goal requires change from everyone in the entire family. The Stepfamily Cycle describes how this happens over time.

The stepfamily life cycle

Seven stages of development for stepfamilies have been identified. In the Early Stages, 1. Fantasy, 2. Immersion, and 3. Awareness, the family remains divided along biological lines, with the closest relationships remaining within biological parent/child "mini-families." In the Middle Stages, 4. Mobilization, and 5. Action, the family structure begins to unfreeze and shift. In the Later Stages, 6. Contact, and 7. Resolution, the new stepfamily solidifies with reliable, nourishing step-relationships, particularly in the couple.

"Fast" families make it through the entire cycle within about four years. "Average" families take about seven years. While seven years, (even four years) may seem like a long time, it is the first four stages that are the uphill part of the cycle. In fact, it is important to note that the differences between families seem to lie primarily in the amount of time it takes families to negotiate the Early Stages. Fast families seem to take about a year. Average families take three to four years. "Stuck" families remain in the Early Stages for more than five years, often moving to divorce. Having gotten through the Early Stages, most families take two or three years to negotiate the Middle Stages, and another year to complete the Later Stages.

The Early Stages: getting started or stuck.

Stage One: fantasy, or the invisible burden.
Every new relationship begins with fantasies about what it will be like, what needs it will meet, what old hurts it will heal. People in stepfamilies come to their lives together with a history of loss that provides a distinct twist to the myths and dreams they bring to stepfamily living. They usually also come with only the experience of biological family living, which can cruelly distort expectations of what is possible in the early years of creating a stepfamily.

Looking back, adult stepfamily members may remember shared fantasies of rescuing children from the excesses or inadequacies of a previous spouse ("Their mother never knit or baked for them, won't they be thrilled with what I can offer.") or making a broken family whole again ("We'd been half a family for so long, I remember thinking we'd be whole again."). For stepparents, the fantasy is often: "I love my new partner, so of course I'll love his/her kids." For biological parents, it is: "I'm so glad to have a new mother/father for my children." And, "I adore him — of course they will love me, too." For members of double families, it is: "Won't my son/daughter be thrilled to live with another child his/her age." For mental health professionals, the fantasy is: "We understand this, so it won't be a problem for us."

Children's fantasies are markedly different. Simply, children want their "real" parents back together again. At the very least they would like the special relationship with their single parent back. As one teenager said candidly, "I thought maybe if I just didn't pay attention to him, the new guy would go away."

Stage Two: immersion, or lost in reality.

One of the cruelest terms we have created for stepfamilies is the phrase "blended family." Most of us know they don't blend. In the Immersion stage, the fantasies of a whole new family and nourishing new stepparent/stepchild relationships begin to rub up against reality. A family used to neatly folded dry towels finds itself living with a family who drops them on the wet floor. A father who has created a tradition of sitting down to meals with his teenagers finds himself married to a woman who eats on the run. While these may seem like small details, they are the threads that hold together the fabric of our lives. Just as in a tapestry, those threads become background in our everyday living. Early stepfamily living puts them all up for grabs. And it feels like life is unraveling.

Furthermore, as stepfamilies begin living together, the reality of a family's structure and history begins to surface.

Even children who had originally welcomed a stepparent find themselves upset and anxious. What adults may see as bad behavior is often, for children, an attempt to deal with some very real problems: loss and loyalty. While the new family is seen as a gain by adults, children see it as one more in a series of losses over which they have no control. Divorce (and the death of a parent) is devastating to children. Children root their sense of self in both parents, and when parents split (even if one has been abusive or cruel) the children feel torn at their very cores. Hard-fought custody battles or one parent's bad mouthing the other often make this more painful for kids.

The close parent-child relationships of the single-parent family offer some solace against this loss, particularly if the parents avoid saying demeaning things about each other to their children. The presence of a new stepparent, however, bumps the child out of this relationship and requires yet one more set of adjustments. Evenings that had been spent cuddling with dad and eating popcorn are spent with a babysitter. Habits that are comfortable and comforting to children are experienced as foreign and irritating to new stepparents (and vice versa).

In addition, adults eager to "blend" their new families often want to pressure children to treat their new stepparents as "mom" or "dad," placing children in an unbearable loyalty bind — "If I love my stepdad, then what about my dad? If I let my stepmother in, haven't I betrayed my mom?" A noncustodial mom or dad who is alcoholic, abusive or otherwise seen as "inadequate" may actually intensify the bind for children who often feel protective of and responsible for a "weak" parent.

It is worth saying that children must be coaxed gently out

of the close relationship with their parents in order for the new stepcouple to succeed. The couple must spend regular time together without children. However, the coaxing needs to be done with awareness of the children's needs. Children need empathy for their feelings, and they need regular and reliable special time with their biological parents. They also need support for their relationships with the nonresidential parent. And, while it is fair to ask a child to be civil to stepparents, it is not fair to expect children to love them.

For stepparents, immersion in stepfamily living makes the pain of their outside position felt. Intimate times with a spouse are interrupted by the children. Children's interruptions are experienced as intimate contact by the biological parent, but as exclusion by the stepparent. Children who were friendly before a marriage can become surly and rejecting. The fantasy of a new marriage recedes as the stepparent tries to make a new couple relationship in the presence of a more intimate, more enduring, and more powerful parent/child relationship. Long held vacation plans are spoiled when the ex-spouse finds a new lover and changes the visitation schedule.

The outsider position places stepparents in the grips of powerful negative feelings: jealousy, resentment, inadequacy and just plain loneliness. These are nobody's favorites, and they are hard to acknowledge. And they hardly ever get support. Stepparents in the immersion stage are often confused and lost, carrying a strong sense that "something's not right here, but I can't figure out what it is." The flood of negative feelings and lack of intimate support often leads to the conclusion "It must be me." In the Early stages, the "insider" position gives biological parents access to both their children and their new partner (as well as to ex-spouses, at times). Established rules and rituals are comfortable and familiar. While this central position becomes increasingly uncomfortable as the family approaches the Middle stages (and the stepparent gains a stronger voice), it provides some measure of comfort at this stage, often allowing the biological parent to hold onto the fantasies of making close stepparent/child relationships for much longer than the stepparent.

Stage Three: awareness, or making sense out of things.

At first tentatively, and then with more confidence, stepfamily members can begin to make more sense out of what is happening to them. Stepparents begin putting names on painful feelings, as well as understanding their sources. "It's not that I get jealous because I'm neurotic; it's because when we're about to make love, the one time of day we have alone, in comes little Emmie to snuggle and I sit there watching." The pain doesn't go away, but the picture of where it comes from gets clearer.

For the biological parent, the reality that "all is not as I wished" often becomes more obvious. It becomes obvious that relationships between stepparents and stepchildren are not going according to fantasy. The central position that has provided some protection from discomfort becomes a form of stress. Biological parents naturally want to protect their children from further hurt and from too much additional change. On the other hand, intimacy with a new partner requires excluding children and imposing new rules. The task of resolving the relationship with the previous spouse may not yet be finished, yet the new couple relationship creates pressure to move on. Adults in difficult ex-spouse relationships often fear that even desirable changes in the ex-spouse relationship could jeopardize financial support or access to the children, while new spouses may experience the unwillingness to make those changes as a lack of commitment or caring.

For stepparents moving from, "Something's wrong here and it must be my fault," to "Something's wrong here and I don't like it," is not an easy task. Stepparents often need support to make that move. The best source of support is a spouse who understands and can listen. "I understand that you're jealous. I'd feel left out too." "I did see Johnny turn his back when you came into the room; that would make me feel bad also."

What distinguishes "fast" families from the rest is that support and understanding on these issues comes from within the couple relationship right from the beginning. However, the "fast" families are also by far in the minority for most stepparents. One's partner is not a reliable source of support on step issues until the Action stage. A biological parent who spent years in a bad marriage, then as a single parent yearning for a "whole" family, may experience the stepparent's jealousy, different feelings toward the children and resulting difficulty relating to them as a lack of desire to be part of the family. This frightening possibility would mean another loss or failure.

John, a biological father, talks about how hard it was for him to bear his new wife Melinda's discomfort: "The thought that Melinda and my daughter wouldn't get along was too painful to even imagine. When Melinda was jealous, I just thought she was being immature. When she was resentful, I thought she was overreacting. I really had no idea what she felt until she dragged me into a stepcouples' group."

Fear and a different experience of how the family is

functioning may combine to make it likely that the biological parent will greet the stepparent's tentative expression of discomfort with disbelief or criticism.

Likewise, a stepparent struggling to maintain self-esteem in the face of powerful negative feelings often does not have enough emotional generosity to understand that his or her partner is in equal, but different, pain. Just as biological parents in the "fast" families are able to empathize with their partner's struggles, stepparents are able to sympathize with the fear and discomfort their concerns elicit and can hang in to help their partners hear them.

In most families, understanding what is happening is talked about only tentatively within the family. Often the stepparent remains the person who is most uncomfortable. Most stepparents need to look for their initial support from outside the family, from a friendship with another stepparent, from reading, from a therapist who understands. It is, at this point in stepfamily development, that I think **STEPFAMILY ASSOCIATION OF AMERICA** helps lower the divorce rate in stepfamilies by providing support and information not yet available from inside the family in the Early stages.

Help in the Early stages.

It is not surprising that many stepfamilies get stuck in the Early stages. There are things we can do that make a difference. The first is to learn as much as possible about stepfamily functioning. Just as no parent relishes temper tantrums, no stepcouple enjoys facing the fact that one is an "insider" and one is an "outsider" any time they are dealing with a child in the Early stages. However, like a two year old's temper tantrums, the problem is not how to avoid this difference, but how to live well with it. Stepparents particularly need support and understanding and a place to vent during this period. Biological parents need to take comfort in the knowledge that listening and trying to understand probably is the thing that will most speed the stepparent's comfort in the new family.

While few children welcome stepfamily living, adults can do much to ease the transition. First and foremost, adults must confine their negative comments about a child's absent parent to private, adult-only conversations. A child in a loyalty bind is a child who will make stepfamily living miserable for everyone. Likewise, children and stepparents need time to get to know each other.

Fulltime stepmothers, in particular, are often expected to step directly into a parenting and disciplinary role, an expectation that is unfair to both stepmother and stepchildren. In general, the biological parent needs to retain disciplinary and primary parenting roles in the Early stages, with the stepparent having input through the biological parent. When the stepparent is in charge in the biological parent's absence, the role is much like a babysitter's — I'm in charge here while your mom or dad is gone, and it's my job to take care of you and enforce the family rules in his/her absence.

Children also need help coping with loss — loss of the original family, loss of a close single-parent/child relationship, and often loss of friends, familiar places and teachers. The best help is time spent really listening to children's feelings without explaining them away.

Listening means putting yourself in the child's shoes, trying to feel what it would feel like, telling the child what you understand, and asking about what you don't understand. As parents it is often difficult to fully face that our actions have hurt our children, and we often feel moved to explain away our children's hurts, "Oh, this is a better school system. " "Your stepfather really does care for you." "You can see your old friends at vacation time." While all of these things may be true, these statements often comfort adults more than children.

What comforts children is to know the adults in their lives understand. "Yeah, this is a brand new school with a brand new teacher." "How is it different?" "That must be hard." "Yes it must be hard dealing with a new adult in this family — it's one more change you didn't ask for." "Yeah, you must miss your old friends." When children yell, "You're not my real parent," I urge stepparents to say, "Yes, you are absolutely right. And it's going to take time for us to get to know each other, and it's really hard for both of us. And then we may still not like each other. Meanwhile, we do have to find a better way to live."

By the end of the early stages of stepfamily development, people in stepfamilies, particularly the stepparent, are much clearer about who they are, what they like and what they don't like about the way their new family works. This sets the stage for a more open airing of differences between the step and biological experiences in the family.

The Middle Stages: reorganizing the family.

Stage Four: mobilization, or airing differences.

This stage could also be called "rocking the boat versus jumping ship." Most stepparents can name a time when they decided to take a stand with their spouse or stepchildren and stick by it — speaking up with more energy and strength about what they needed and how they saw things. The particular issues around which stepparents recall mobilizing themselves vary tremendously. Some finally insist on a lock on the parental bedroom. Some lobby vigorously for a particular rule change. Some fulltime stepmothers remember "resigning," stepping back and insisting that their husbands reclaim their disciplinary and nurturing roles with their own children. One stepfather remembers finally holding his ground about late-night phonecalls from his wife's ex-husband.

The initiators of fights in this phase are the people in the family who are feeling most excluded, dissatisfied and uncomfortable. Usually it is the stepparent. Sometimes it is a child. While it is easy to frame the person who starts the fight as a "troublemaker," in fact, that should be welcomed. They are the family change agents — the people willing to rock the boat enough to make everyone pay attention to the fact that things are not terrific in this stepfamily, and that the family needs to work together to make some changes.

In some families, the stepparent's request is received with relieved support by the biological parent who is thrilled to know what she or he can do to make the new spouse more comfortable. In many families, however, the stepparent's more vigorous stance ushers in a period of conflict and chaos. It also makes life much harder for the biological parent, who begins to feel torn between the needs of his or her new spouse and the need to protect children from further disruptive change.

It is important to remember during this phase that while the issues we fight over may seem trivial (whole wheat versus white bread; 10 or 11 o'clock bedtime; Is it OK to eat buttered toast in the living room?), they are actually major struggles over whose needs for comfort and intimacy will be met. These struggles also help define whether the biological mini-family will continue to function as it has or change its structure. These fights are intense because they take place at the heart of our family life — around issues that touch the core of our selves — the need for intimacy and understanding.

The temptation, and the pitfall, is to assume that someone is right and someone is wrong. Couples navigate beyond this stage when they finally begin to realize that, in fact, each person in the family is in pain over these differences. Some stepcouples find they can steer their way through these conflicts by simply hanging in and talking.

Jim, a biological father and stepfather in a "double" family, described it this way: "Well, we were living in North Carolina at the time. In North Carolina the weather is real warm a lot. And we sat out on the back patio and confronted each other a lot. It wasn't always pretty, but even though it was hard, we knew it was important, and we had enough good will that we didn't tear our relationship apart while we were fighting. We talked and talked until we figured out what to do."

Many couples find they cannot fight openly without tearing their relationships apart. The pull to return to the more silent discomfort of the Early stages is powerful. For most couples, this is a good time to get some help. Ask everyone you know who they've heard is a good empathic couple or family therapist who knows about stepfamilies. It is particularly important that you find a therapist who is able to empathize with all of the people in your family. Empathy is in short supply in stepfamilies at this stage, and it is often easier for a therapist to understand one family member at the expense of understanding another. Attend meetings of your local **STEP-FAMILY ASSOCIATION OF AMERICA** Chapter, often referred to as **STEPFAMILIES**. Find a stepcouples' group. You are doing something hard, and you need all the support you can get.

Stage Five: action, or going into business together.

The energy and expressiveness of the Mobilization stage begins to loosen up the old biological family structure, making way for building a new one, as couples work together to resolve their differences.

To do this well, it is as if the couple must travel back to the Awareness stage (stage three) and talk and listen long enough to understand each other's very different experiences. Most workable solutions that result from this effort will meet some of each person's needs. Often the solution will leave some of the "old" ways of doing things intact, while inventing something brand new.

While couples may still be fighting in this phase, the difference is that the fights get finished, and a decision is made that addresses some of the needs of each of the players in the drama. Fights in the Early Stages rarely gained much momentum, with most decisions being one-sided (usually supporting the status quo). Fights in the Mobilization stage may be lively but have no resolution. In the Action phase, it is as if both members of the couple are on the same side, trying to figure out how to balance a complex set of needs and feelings.

Furthermore, the decisions in this phase actually change the family structure and way of functioning. Most important, the couple begins to carve out time and space together and begins to evolve a way to work together to solve step issues. A typical problem, for instance, was Tom and Jenny's: What to do about the fact that Jenny (the stepmother) finds weekends with Ricky (the eight year old stepson) exhausting. Tom (Ricky's dad) wants the whole family to be together. Jenny is exhausted from working all week and really just wants time alone with Tom or by herself. Ricky wants his dad to himself. In the Immersion stage, (stage two), the weekend visits went on in an atmosphere of tension and anxiety, with Jenny blaming herself for her inability to enjoy herself and Tom feeling abandoned by her apparent distance. In the Mobilization stage, they fought over who was more inadequate — Jenny for being so anxious, or Tom for being so rigid. In the Action Stage, Jenny and Tom sat down and figured out a way to make the weekends work better.

Tom would pick up Ricky without Jenny (previously they had all gone together, and Jenny sat in the back seat listening to Tom and Ricky talk, feeling left out, exhausted, resentful, and inadequate). This way, Tom and Ricky would have time alone together, and Jenny would have some time to herself on Saturday morning. Tom and Ricky would return in the early afternoon for some family time. Sometime during the evening, Tom and Jenny would go for a walk, just the two of them, and Tom promised to put his arm around her and look straight at her at least once a day while Ricky was with them. In addition, Tom and Jenny would have an intimate "date" on the Thursday nights before weekends with Ricky. Now they can afford to go out for dinner, but when they were poor, it was pizza and watching Hill Street Blues together, cuddled in bed. The new plan made for much smoother, easier weekends for all concerned.

Just as establishing a workable stepcouple relationship requires gently coaxing the child out to make time alone for adults, the stepparent-stepchild relationship cannot flourish until the biological parent begins to move out of the way and allows stepparent and stepchild to work things out together. The biological parent may need to learn to stay in the background when stepparent and stepchild are engaged in a game. The stepparent may need to learn to remind the biological parent to bite his or her tongue when stepparent and stepchild are fighting.

Unlike in the Early Stages, where stepparents need to allow biological parents to make most of the disciplinary moves, it is time for the stepparent to begin moving into the disciplinary role by the end of the Action stage — taking a few issues at a time, with the biological parent backing the stepparent up (and handling disagreements about rules in private adult time). The trick is to work together to invent rules that balance the needs of all members of the family and to balance the stepparent's need for change with the biological mini-family's need for stability.

While the start of the Middle Stages can be quite frightening, it may help to remember that if you are airing differences, you are halfway there. At least things are out in the open.

There are two things that help couples move from Mobilization to Action — joining and strategic planning. "Joining" means empathizing. It doesn't mean giving up your point of view. It does mean taking a moment before you respond to imagine what the other person must be feeling and saying it aloud to them. Most of us spend our time while another person is talking figuring out how to make our own points. The problem is that the harder I make my point, the less heard and seen you feel. And the less heard and seen you feel, the harder I make my point. On and on we go, until we're both thoroughly convinced that the other is a villain. On the most practical level, joining means saying back to your spouse (or your child) the essence of what you think he or she was trying to say, each time, before responding with something new of your own. While it sounds simple, it is hard to do. And yet it makes a tremendous difference in keeping each other open while you are disagreeing with each other.

"Strategic planning" means just what it says. It means sitting down as a team with all the information you have available about what everyone wants and needs and figuring out a creative way to meet as many needs as possible.

Fighting for one side to win and the other to lose makes strategic planning impossible. Tom and Jenny's strategic weekend plan came out of assuming that their needs were equal, but different. Had they assumed that one would win and the other would lose, no such plan could have been invented, and their weekends would have continued miserably.

Stepfamilies end the Middle Stages having moved from being a biological mini-family with a stepparent outsider (or two biological mini-families living side by side) to a stepfamily run by a stepcouple team.

The Later Stages: solidifying the stepfamily

By the end of the Middle Stages, it is as if the stepfamily has built new walls in its house — to create a new room for the couple without children, and often new rooms for the stepparents and stepchildren without the biological parent. In the Later Stages, it is time for the effort of building new rooms to fade into the background, leaving energy and attention for furnishing and living in them.

Stage Six: contact, or intimacy in step relationships

The changes of the Action phase ease children out of the adult couple relationship and ease the biological parent out of the stepparent-child relationship, making it possible for people in step-relationships to begin to really get to know each other.

The stepparent and stepchild have heart-to-heart talks more often than their previous hit-and-run conversations. Fights that had been left hanging uncomfortably in the early stages are now fought to a satisfying finish. Most important, the adult couple relationship, which had been so easily polarized by step issues begins to be a more intimate sanctuary to which we can bring our feelings and problems.

It is in the Contact Stage that stepparents can first confidently describe solid, workable stepparent roles. It is no accident that this does not happen until after the restructuring moves of the Action phase, and after the biological parent and stepparent begin to understand each other's very different experiences and work as a team. The very differences that caused great discomfort and conflict in previous stages of the stepfamily may now form the foundation of the stepparent's role in the family. For example, an expressive man who entered a very polite and careful family becomes "the one around here who teaches us about feelings." An organized and highly self-disciplined woman who married a hang-loose mini-family becomes "the one who holds things together around here."

Stage Seven: resolution, or holding on and letting go.

So what do stepfamilies look like when they've "made it"? By the Resolution stage, most of the hardest, uphill work is behind the family. Step-relationships are no longer uncertain territory, but provide a solid background to the family's functioning. Norms and rules have been established, the problem of the wet towels is far in the background, new rituals have begun to be built. Someone in the family can say, "we do things this way here," and rather than creating tension (as in the Early stages), or starting a war (as in the Middle Stages), most people will agree.

Issues that had caused panic in the past are simply normal events. Joanna describes it this way: "It used to be that Gabriel's middle son Danny would call to speak with his father, and he wouldn't even say hello to me. For a long time, I just handed the phone to Gabriel and didn't say a word. But it hurt so badly. I felt so inadequate. For awhile after that, I worked on Gabriel to make his son talk to me. Now I just let it go by. Danny is very close to his mother, who is still bitter about the divorce. Maybe when Danny moves out of the house, he'll be free to get to know me. For now, I just tell Gabriel, and he gives me a hug and I don't even think about it again."

Not all children in a family move at the same pace. For instance, when Joanne divorced her husband, her son Jimmy was three and her daughter Jenna was eight. Three years later, when Joanne married Gabriel, who had three teenage sons, her son Jimmy and Gabriel "hit it off from the start," while Jenna had a much more difficult time. Likewise, eight years later, Joanna is quite close to one of Gabriel's sons, has a working relationship with another, and remains "really at square one" with his middle son. What makes or breaks stepfamilies is the couple relationship. As long as that works, the rest is workable.

Although some children may not yet (and may never be) part of the new family, most stepparent-child relationships feel solid and reliable. One stepfather put it eloquently and simply, "deep down, I really know now that my stepdaughter and I have a very special connection that can't be threatened by anything. And I know it is a lifetime connection. And there is a real bottom line of security there where I know I have already made a big difference to her, and I know she's made a big difference to me."

One of the most satisfying parts of the Resolution stage for stepparents is the experience of a mature, satisfying stepparent role. Stepparents now find themselves in a very special role, as an "intimate outsider" — intimate enough to be privy to important details of their stepchildren's lives, and distant enough to be confidants for the "really good stuff": sexuality, drug use, unresolved feelings about the divorce, etc.

New step issues continue to arise in these complicated families: attendance at weddings and graduations, money for college, the desire of a childless stepparent for an "ours" baby. While particularly stressful issues may temporarily throw the whole family back to an earlier stage, most occur within the context of a solid couple and stepfamily structure whose members trust each other, and expect each other to be there and know they'll work it out eventually.

The result is a family that has built "bonds without blood," bonds that are incredibly rich and strong because they had to be created on purpose. Couples who have learned to work well together over step issues find other issues "a breeze by comparison." "It's sort of like climbing an especially high mountain. The climb has its hard parts, but the feeling at the top is exhilarating and leaves an incredible feeling of mastery and confidence, even years later."

"The Stepfamily Cycle" by Patricia Papernow originally appeared in the *Stepfamily Bulletin* (Fall and Winter 1986). It has been reprinted with permission of the author.

GUIDELINES FOR STEPFAMILIES

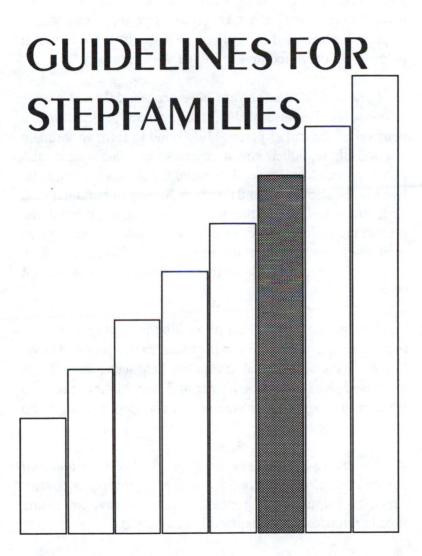

Guidelines for stepfamilies

1. It is difficult to have a new person or persons move into your "space," and it is difficult to be the "new" person or people joining a preexisting group. For these reasons, if stepfamilies can start out in their own apartment or house, it helps to cut down feelings involved with "territory."

2. Parent-child relationships have preceded the new couple relationship. Because of this, many parents feel that it is a betrayal of the earlier parent-child bond to form an intimate relationship with their new partner. An intimate couple relationship, however, is usually crucial for the continuing existence of the stepfamily, and therefore, is very important for the children as well as for the adults. A strong adult bond can protect the children from another family loss and strengthen their own eventual marriage relationship. The adults often need to arrange time alone to help nourish this important couple relationship.

3. Forming new relationships within the stepfamily can be important, particularly when the children are young. Activities involving different subgroups can help such relationships to grow. For example, stepfather and stepchildren might do some project together; or stepmother and stepchild might go shopping together.

4. Preserving original relationships is also important and can help children experience less loss at sharing a parent. Thus, it is helpful for a parent and children to have some time together in addition to stepfamily activities.

5. *Caring relationships take time to evolve.* The expectation of "instant love" or even "instant friendship" between stepparents and stepchildren can lead to many disappointments and difficulties. If the stepfamily relationships are allowed to develop as seem comfortable to the individuals involved, then friendship and caring between step-relatives has the opportunity to develop.

6. *Stepfamilies are structurally and emotionally different from first families.* Upset and sadness is experienced by the children and, at times, by the adults as they react to the loss of their original family or to the loss of a dream of a perfect marriage. Acceptance that a stepfamily is a different type of family is important, as is the recognition that many upsetting behaviors result from these feelings of insecurity and loss.

7. *Because children are a product of two biological parents, they nearly always have very strong pulls to both of these natural parents.* These divided loyalties often make it difficult for children to relate comfortably to all the parental adults in their lives. Rejection of a stepparent, for example, may have nothing to do with the personal characteristics of the stepparent. In fact, warm and loving stepparents may cause especially severe loyalty conflicts for children. As children and adults are able to accept the fact that children can care for more than two parental adults, then the children's loyalty conflicts can diminish and the new step-relationships improve. While it may be helpful to the children for the adults to acknowledge negative as well as positive feelings about ex-spouses, children may become caught in loyalty conflicts and feel personally insecure if specific critical remarks are made continously

about their other biological parent.

8. *Courteous relationships between ex-spouses are important, although they are very difficult for many adults to maintain.* If such a relationship can be worked out, it is especially helpful to the children. In such instances, the children do not get caught in the middle between two hostile parents, there is less need for the children to take sides, and the children are better able to accept and utilize the positive elements in their living and visiting arrangements. Direct contact between the adults can be helpful since it does not place the children in the sometimes powerful position of being message carriers between their biological parents. Although it may be strained, many ex-spouses are able to relate if the focus is kept on their mutual concern for the welfare of the children.

9. *Children as well as adults in a stepfamily have a "family history."* Suddenly these individuals come together and their sets of "givens" are questioned. Much is to be gained by coming together as a stepfamily unit to work out and develop new family patterns and traditions. Even when the individuals are able to recognize that patterns are not "right" or "wrong," it takes time and patience to work out satisfying new alternatives.

Values (the underlying approach to life and general ways of doing things) do not shift easily. Within a stepfamily, different value systems are inevitable because of different previous family histories, and tolerance for these differences can help smooth the process of stepfamily integration. Needs (specific ways individuals relate together, individual preferences, etc.) can usually be negotiated more quickly than can general values. Having an appreciation for and an expectation of such difficulties can make for more flexibility and relaxation in the stepfamily unit. Negotiation and renegotiation are needed by most such families.

10. Being a stepparent is an unclear and at times difficult task. The wicked stepmother myth contributes to the discomfort of many women, and cultural, structural and personal factors affect the stepparent role. Spouses can be very helpful to one another if they are able to be supportive with the working out of new family patterns. Stepparenting is usually more successful if stepparents carve out a role for themselves that is different from and does not compete with the biological parents.

While discipline is not usually accepted by stepchildren until a friendly relationship has been established (often a matter of 18 to 24 months or more), both adults do need to support each other's authority in the household. The biological parent may be the primary disciplinarian initially, but when that person is unavailable, it is often necessary for that parent to give a clear message to the children that the stepparent is acting as an "authority figure" for both adults in his or her absence.

Unity between the couple is important to the functioning of the stepfamily. When the couple is comfortable with each other, differences between them in regards to the children can sometimes be worked out in the presence of the children, but at no time does it work out for either children or adults to let the children approach each adult separately and "divide and conquer." When disciplinary action is necessary, if it is not kept within the stepfamily household, many resentful feelings can be generated. For example, if visitation rights are affected, the noncustodial parent is being included in the action without his or her representation. Such a punishment, then, may lead to difficulties greater than the original behavior that caused the disciplinary action.

11. Integrating a stepfamily that contains teenagers can be particularly difficult. At this age, adolescents are moving away from their families in any type of family. In single parent families, teenagers have often been "young adults," and with the remarriage of a parent, they may find it extremely difficult or impossible to return to being in a "child" position.

Adolescents have more of a previous "family history" and so they ordinarily appreciate having considerable opportunity to be part of the stepfamily negotiations, although they may withdraw from both biological parents and not wish to be part of many of the "family activities."

12. "Visiting" children usually feel strange and are outsiders in the neighborhood. It can be helpful it they have some place in the household that is their own (for example, if not a room, a drawer or a shelf for toys and clothes). If they are included in stepfamily chores and projects when they are with the stepfamily, they tend to feel more connected to the group. Bringing a friend with them to share the visit and having some active adult participation in becoming integrated into the neighborhood can make a difference to many visiting children. Knowing ahead of time that there is going to be an interesting activity, stepfamily game of monopoly, etc., can sometimes give visiting children a pleasant activity to anticipate.

Noncustodial parents and stepparents often are concerned because they have so little time to transmit their values to visiting children. Since children tend to resist concerted efforts by the adults to instill stepfamily ideals during each visit, it is comforting to parents and stepparents to learn that examples of behavior and relationships simply observed in the household can affect choices made by all the children later in their lives when they are grown and on their own.

13. Sexuality is usually more apparent in stepfamilies because of the new couple relationship, and because children may suddenly be living with other children with whom they have not grown up. There also are not the usual incest taboos in operation. It is important for the children to receive affection and to be aware of tenderness between the couple, but it may also be important for the couple to minimize to some extent the sexual aspects of the household and to help the children understand, accept, and control their sexual attraction to one another or to the adults.

14. All families experience stressful times. Children tend to show little day-to-day appreciation for their stepparents and, at times, they get angry and reject their biological parents. Because stepfamilies are families born of loss, the mixture of feelings can be even more intense than in first marriage families. Jealousy, rejection, guilt, and anger can be more pronounced, and, therefore, expectations that the stepfamily will live "happily ever after" are even more unrealistic than in first families. Having an understanding and acceptance of the many negatives as well as positive feelings can result in less disappointment and more stepfamily enjoyment.

15. Keeping even minimal contact between adults and children can lead to future satisfaction since time and maturity bring many changes. With some communication between stepfamily members, satisfying interpersonal relationships often develop in the future when children become more independent in their relationships with both biological parents and with stepparents.

(Printed with permission from Stepfamilies: A Guide to Working with Stepparents and Stepchildren, by Emily B. Visher and John S Visher, New York: Brunner/Mazel, 1979.)

THE STEPPING AHEAD PROGRAM

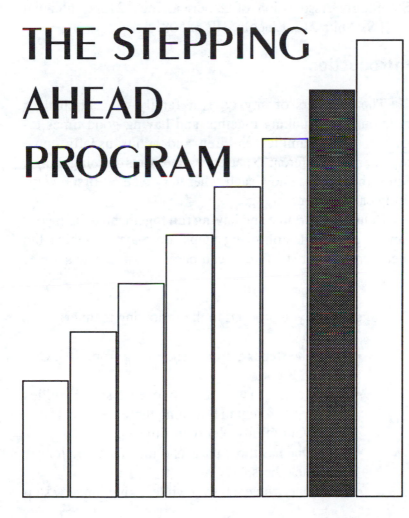

Stepping ahead:
A program for successful family living.

If you are interested in starting a support group or a chapter based on this program, a leader's manual is available from Stepfamily Association of America, Inc., 215 Centennial Mall S., Suite 212, Lincoln, NE 68508.

Introduction

The members of any type of family can enrich their relationship by talking together and having good times together. In stepfamilies children and adults usually come together with different experiences and ways of doing things. Since they do not know each other very well, at first, everything can feel very strange.

Being comfortable and having fun together can help your family grow. The following steps are ways in which the members of your stepfamily can begin to know one another better.

We suggest that you proceed in the following manner:

- Take the steps in order proceeding from Step One to Step Eight.
- Allow at least a week or two for each step. Families are very different in how long these steps will take. Give your family plenty of time.
- Step One has three parts and may take you longer than the others.
- Continue with each step while taking the new step

(for example, continue with Steps One and Two while going on to Step Three).

- Go on to another step if you get stuck on any one of them. All families are different, and you may find that the steps do not go from easier to harder for you.
- If you have supportive friends or a stepfamily support group, share with them the things that have worked or not worked for you as you climb these steps. You can receive good ideas from them, and they can benefit from your experience.

Step One: Nurturing your couple relationship

An important task for the two adults in a stepfamily household is to see that their relationship continues to grow and develop. This is important because it can:

- Enrich the lives of both of the adults.
- Enable your household to remain together so that all of you do not experience another period of separation and upset.
- Help the two of you work together as a team.
- Develop your leadership as a couple. This is necessary so that children feel secure that there are adults who will take care of them. It provides your children with a model of adults who care about each other and can work out family challenges in productive ways. Having had such a model is extremely beneficial to your children when they mature and form their own couple relationships.

A. Plan to do something away from your household once a week that you both enjoy doing together

- You will probably need to plan ahead for this since time for such activities seldom arises spontaneously in a busy household.
- If you have not yet developed common interests you may need to take turns choosing the activities. This allows each of you to experience what the other enjoys and paves the way for you to discover what interests you may wish to pursue together.
- A few suggested activities that couples have enjoyed:

Taking a walk	Visiting friends
Going to a movie	Going to the beach
Going out for coffee	Playing golf or tennis
Visiting a museum	Playing cards
Going out for dinner	Horseback riding
Going skating	Sitting in the park

- If you have young children and do not have the money for a baby sitter, trading child care hours with another couple (or forming a child care "cooperative" with several other couples) can benefit everyone.
- You may need to make a rule that you do not discuss family problems at these times of "rest and relaxation." Without this rule it is easy to slip into discussions or arguments about family matters. This subtracts from the internal nourishment you need to receive from these periods of freedom.

B. Arrange to have 20 minutes of relaxed time alone with each other every day

- Couples can relax together while:

Talking a walk	Watching TV
Getting ready for bed	Talking
Cooking	Listening to music
Gardening	Reading in the same room

- Sleeping in the same bed doesn't count.
- Subtract two points for arguing in bed!
- Snuggling, being intimate, or talking together in bed counts double!
- You may need to barricade the door against forced entry by the children.

OR

- Put up a sign that says "Do not knock unless you're bleeding." Seriously, it is important for the parent of the child or children to see that his/her children respect the privacy needs of the couple (and, in return, that the adults respect the privacy needs of the children).

C. Talk together about the running of your household for at least 30 minutes each week

- Settle on three major things that you both agree are important to the household and let other matters go.

Maybe other things can be changed later on if needed.

- Choose things that can be clearly understood and are within the realm of possibility! Some examples of things that have been important to couples are:

    Finishing homework before watching TV.
    Using good table manners at dinner.
    Leaving muddy shoes on the back porch.
    Taking turns washing and drying the dishes.
    Not eating or drinking in the living room.

- There may need to be different regulations when there are more or fewer people together (if children go between households).

- House rules need to apply to you as well as to your children. This helps the children feel that you are being fair.

- The parent of the child or children needs to be the person to see that the rule is followed, while the stepparent needs to back up the parent.

- If the stepparent is to be alone with the stepchild or children, the parent needs to call everyone together and tell the children that the stepparent is in charge when he/she is not there (the way you would do it when you have a child care person coming in).

- When the stepparent has been in charge, the parent needs to back up the stepparent when he/she returns. (As stepparents and stepchildren get to know one another better, the stepparents will be able to share this "management" responsibility with the parent more and more of the time.)

Step Two: Finding personal space and time

As a rule, stepfamilies have more people in them than there are in other kinds of families. This means that it may be difficult for stepfamily members to have the space and time for themselves that they would like to have.

A special place of one's own, and "alone" time can be necessary:

- to feel that there's room for you in the household.
- to find needed relaxation and feel refreshed.
- to know you have a private spot of your own even if you are not always living in the household.

A. Take time to make a special "private" place for each of the adults and children in your household.

Work with each other to figure out what space can be created for each person. The following are ideas that have worked for stepfamily members when rooms need to be shared in their home:

A drawer for children who come on weekends.
A small shed or room in the backyard.
Part of a closet.
A special shelf.
A low divider in a room.
A corner of the garage remodeled.
An attic or basement hideaway.
A tree house.
Bunk beds that divide a room.

- The "owner" of each space has control over that place. It is a private spot for that person, and no one may intrude without permission of the owner.
- What people do with their space is up to them. Private space is also not used to store household items (e.g. brooms, clothes, laundry equipment) or things belonging to others.
- Find a way to ensure that the space created for children who are not in the household all the time will remain "off limits" to others when they are not present. This may require a lock, a high latch, or clearly understood (and followed) consequences if this private place is invaded by another person.
- If a whole room or work space is available (bedroom, sewing room, workshop, darkroom, music room, etc.), this space is treated similarly to the more limited space just discussed.

B. Each take two hours a week doing something for yourselves that you would like to do.

Unfortunately, as we grow older we do not always give ourselves and other family members "permission" to spend time doing things that are personally pleasurable for us. This greatly reduces our enjoyment of life and actually can make us harder to live with.

- Your special time may be spent in your personal space or it may be spent somewhere else. For example:
  Walking   Visiting with friends

Having a massage	Reading
Bowling	Sewing
Going shopping	Watching TV
Woodworking	Going to the beautician

- Let other family members know when you are planning these personal times.
- Do not interrupt one another during these special personal times.
- Help your partner and your children respect your time to be alone by taking a few minutes to see if they need anything from you before you go off by yourself.
- Give the others in your household two or three times to get used to your not being "there" for them if they are home at the time.
- Choose times that can work out the most conveniently for you and your family.

When you each feel comfortable doing things each week that you like to do for yourself, and also find that you are able to let your partner do what he/she would like to do, continue to Step Three. Remember to have a good time together as a couple and work together in the way outlined in Step One at the same time that you give yourself and your family personal space and time.

Step Three: Nourishing family relationships

When we feel happy about ourselves, the whole world looks better. One thing that helps people feel good is to be appreciated by others. In families it is easy to pay attention to things that bother us and not notice things that contribute to our comfort. Because of this, family members can feel not appreciated and down on themselves, and then the household isn't a very happy place. The following step is a good way to be sure this is not happening in your family:

Giving positive feedback to one another can:

- create a pleasant family atmosphere.
- help people feel good about themselves.
- build warm feelings between family members.
- make people more aware of things in the family that they like.
- encourage adults and children to repeat the behavior and respond similarly in the future.
- provide a model for good relationships outside, as well as inside, the household.

A. Family members share with one another what they have appreciated about each other

A very good time to do this can be at dinner, but any time the family is together is fine.

- First of all, the two adults tell each other what they have appreciated about each other during the day. (Children like to have the couple go first and listen to what they say to each other.)
- Next, take turns with each two people telling one another what they have appreciated for that day. For

example, mother and son, stepbrother and sister, stepmother and stepdaughter, stepfather and step-son.)

- Having the adults and children share, and then child to child, may be a good order.
- As you start doing this, you will probably notice more and more pleasant times during the day that you will want to acknowledge. For example:

    "Reading me a bedtime story last night."

    "Taking me to the store."

    "Cleaning off the table so quickly."

    "Helping me sweep the front sidewalk."

    "Laughing at the joke I told."

    "Being quiet when Tommie and I were having an argument."

    "Talking to my aunt on the telephone this morning."

    "Not getting mad when I broke the plate."

Mealtime is a common time for family members to be together. Sharing these good feelings with each other helps to make dinner a time that family members enjoy being together. Even young children sense the pleasurable mood.

- Save problem solving for other times.
- If a family member is not able to join the group for dinner, the adults can remember to make appreciative remarks to that person at another time. Children may begin to copy this delightful habit!
- Find a different time to "trade appreciation" if your family is not able to be together for dinner.

When you feel comfortable with this step, go on the Step Four. Keep in mind that paying attention to people's continuing need for appreciation helps with all the other steps.

Step Four: Maintaining Close Parent/Child Relationships

As a rule, in the period between a death or divorce and a parent's remarriage, children have had close to 100% of their parent's attention when they have been together. This ends when a new marriage takes place and there are others now sharing the time and space of the parent. Even though children may want to continue as before, it is usually not possible, nor even in their best interest. They need to have a parent who has remarried to spend time with his/her new partner for the children's sake as well as for the adult's sake (see Step One). The children need to know that they continue to be loved by their parent. When children have this reassurance they:

- accept the new people in the household more easily.
- do not compete as much for their parent's attention.
- do not try to control the situation by misbehavior.
- feel better about themselves.

Step Four is one way to let children know that they continue to have a very special place in their parent's affection. It also helps the parent who may be feeling pulled apart by wanting to please both his/her children and the new partner.

A. Parent and child do something fun together for 15-20 minutes once or twice each week

- If you have several children, you may sometimes do something with them together, but one-on-one time is important even if it comes only once a week.
- If your children are with you only for relatively brief periods, you can spend this 15-20 minute period of time alone with them each day they are with you.
- If you see your children only once or twice a year, do this when they are with you, and in-between send each a letter or telephone them once every two weeks. Make the calls or letters "chatty," unless your child wants to have more serious interchanges.
- It is helpful for your children to plan with you when this contact will be — not so far ahead it seems like "forever" to them, but rather a day or an hour ahead. Then they may be able to share you more easily with others in your household since they know when their time with you is coming.
- Be sure to work out your plans with your partner before you mention them to your child.
- There are many things you and your child can do together for your special time:

Read a bedtime story	Work on a project
Go to the store	Play a game
Cook dinner together	Build sand castles
Play "catch"	Talk together
Ride bicycles	Sail a boat

- These times together do not depend on the behavior of your child. They take place even if your child has misbehaved with any disciplinary actions taking place at a separate time.
- You need to pay particular attention to what your child would like to do. This lets your child know that you care about his/her wishes.
- If you are not able to do what your child would like, do your best to explain why you can't and try to find a good substitute.
- If nothing is satisfactory to your child, give him/her the opportunity to think of other possibilities and let you know when he/she has some further ideas.
- Let your child know at the beginning about how long the two of you will be able to be together in this way. For example:

  "Sure, we can take a bike ride until 4:30."

  "We'll have time for just one game tonight."

  "I can see we won't have time to finish this. We can work on it for ten minutes and then do it again tomorrow."
- If your child wants more time than will work out for you or others in the household you can deal with this by saying something like:

  "Yes, it's hard to stop, but we can do this again (suggest a specific time) if you'd like to."

  "I know you'd like to go on, but I'm not able to right now because (give a reason)."

  "I'm sorry you're feeling so upset about stopping. I know it's hard. When would you like to do it again?"

- Don't try to talk your child out of feelings of upset; simply let him/her know you can understand. Having someone tell you why you should be able to cheer up when that's not how you feel usually makes you feel worse rather than better.
- If your child continues to be upset because there is "never enough time," you may want to share the way this makes you feel. You can say something like:

   "I know it's hard. I like playing with you, but it's no fun for me if you keep crying when we have to stop. It makes me feel that I don't want to do it like this again."

Say this when you are feeling that it's not fun for you if he/she is going to be unhappy with what you can do. Say something like this before you get angry. If you wait until you are angry, then the time together will leave both of you with unhappy, rather than happy, memories.

- If you have more than one child you may need to plan ahead with all of them so that each knows when his/her time is coming.
- If only one of you has children, it is crucial to continue Step One as outlined or your partner will feel left out.
- In all families it is important to share couple time as well as alone time and to continue with positive feedback to one another.

When you feel ready, continue to Step Five.

Step Five: Developing stepparent/stepchild relationships

Stepparents and stepchildren come together knowing little about one another, and usually knowing very little about what it is like being together in a family situation.

Step Five is an excellent way to build good relationships with your stepchildren. This can be valuable because:

- It helps you feel more "inside" the family.
- Your stepchildren will feel happier and enjoy your family more.
- Your partner can be more relaxed because he/she doesn't feel "pulled" between you and your stepchildren.

A. Stepparent and stepchild do something fun together for 15-20 minutes once or twice each week

- As with their parent, if you have several stepchildren you may sometimes do something with them as a group, but one-on-one time is the way to build relationships, so it is important to do something alone with one stepchild at a time at least once a week.
- If your stepchild is with you infrequently, you can do something together for a few minutes each day that the child is there.
- At first it may work out better not to plan the time ahead with your stepchild; instead, slide into it easily at a time you have worked out for yourself

with your partner.

- What you do with your stepchildren may be similar to the things that their parent does with them (see Step Four) or, it may be something different because you are bringing new skills and interests into your stepchildren's lives. Your contacts might include:

    Driving them to school or activities after school.
    Helping with homework.
    Cooking a favorite meal of theirs.
    Taking them shopping.
    Helping them get dressed.
    Teaching them how to ride a bicycle.
    Giving them driving lessons.
    Planning a surprise for their parent.

- As with the special together things the children do with their parent, these times together with your stepchild need to take place whether or not the child has misbehaved. Consequences of misbehavior need to be dealt with by the parent at another time.
- You and your stepchild need to talk together about things you've done in the past that you each liked and didn't like. This will help you get to know one another better, and it will help you decide what would be fun to do together now.
- If your stepchild refuses to do something with you, let it go by saying something like:

    "OK. Maybe we can do it another time."
    "All right. If there's something else you'd like to do, let me know."

- One good way to help your stepchild relate to you is to ask him/her to teach you something. For example:

> "I really like the way you dress. Would you help me figure out what I should wear today?"
> "You are such a good checker player. Would you teach me how to play?"
> "I haven't played hopscotch for so long. Will you show me what you're supposed to do?"

- The parent needs to stay out of the way so that the stepparent can become a part of the stepchild's life. Sometimes it is necessary for the parent to actually be away from the household.

- If you are the parent, you may find it difficult to let your child and your new partner be alone without you. You want them to get along, but it can also make you feel sad not to be the only adult in the household your child or children can turn to. Sometimes it's hard to remember that "There's enough love to go around," to quote one mother/stepmother talking about the feelings of the children. Just because they have several adults to care about doesn't mean that your children will love you any less.

Sometimes it will take a long time to accomplish this step. Even if stepparents are willing to build new relationships, children, particularly teenagers, may not be. Perhaps all you can do now is become involved with your stepchildren by going with their parent to school, functions, sports events, or other activities they take part in. You can also be sure not to leave yourself out of conversations with them at home. If this is the situation in your stepfamily, you may wish to continue on to Step Six and return to this step later. In the meantime, keep this step in the back of your mind so that you will not miss opportunities to get to know your stepchildren better.

Step Six: Building family trust

Relationships and "family feelings" are built on a foundation of trust, and trust comes from having meaningful shared memories. At the beginning of a stepfamily, the group has not been together long enough to have these shared memories. As time passes, trust and the feeling of belonging to the family unit can emerge as individuals talk together, share happy times, and the family develops its own special rituals.

- It is important to have these family times because they help:
  Connect the people who have shared the activity.
  Provide relaxed times to balance intense times.
  Make life enjoyable for the family.
  Give people a feeling of belonging to the family group.
  Build warm memories that are shared.

A. Schedule a family event once a month

- Plan ahead in a manner to include as many family members as possible.
- If you have teenagers, make the "happening" available to them, but let go of the expectation that they will choose to participate. Adolescents tend to prefer activities with their friends, and are moving

away from their parents and are putting energy into forming new relationships. (With an open door policy, when they become adults, they frequently return to relate on an adult-adult basis.)

- When planning for special events such as birthdays and holidays, talk together about past rituals and combine former traditions in creative ways. For example:

    Have creamed onions, mashed potatoes and candied sweet potatoes for Thanksgiving.

    Have a family birthday party and also a party with a group of friends.

    Combine different religious practices.

    Offer candied apples made by everyone as well as sugarless gum on Halloween.

- Discuss new ideas and begin special traditions for your family unit, such as:

    Baking cookies together at Christmas.

    Having a picnic and watching public fireworks on July 4th.

    Playing Monopoly together.

    Going out for pizza on Saturday.

    Having a skiing weekend during the winter school holidays.

    Going to the sneak movie preview on Friday evening.

Take advantage of the many interests your family members may have and plan events with these in mind. Activities enjoyed by families are extremely diverse, including:

Roller skating.
Going to Little League games.
Going to the movies.
Visiting the zoo.
Going to hear popular musical personalities.
Working together in the yard ('tis true — with young children).
Playing miniature golf.
Visiting a local water slide.

A good way to encourage all family members to do something together is to give each person (including young children) a turn deciding what the family will do together for one to one and a half hours twice a month. Everyone needs to participate whether or not it's a familiar activity — if it's not your favorite thing to do, you will have your choice later.

- For example, a family of five might choose the following:

    Teenager — all go out for pizza.
    Four year old — we all color together.
    Adult — we all take a walk in the woods
    Adult — we watch a special TV program together and talk about it.
    Eight year old — we all play "Fish."

- If you have "resident" children and "nonresident" children who are with you more infrequently, plan some events in-between those involving the larger group so that the resident children do not assume that these special family times occur only when nonresident children are in the household.

- Let these special times be separated from consequences for undesirable behavior (except in very unusual circumstances). If this is not done, people's behavior can get worse rather than better because they are not having fun and they begin to feel angry and hopeless.

By the time that your family is having these pleasant times together, you will also be doing nice things alone and in different twosomes (See Steps One through Five) and finding many things you appreciate about one another. When you feel comfortable with these steps, then you will find it helpful to go on to Step Seven.

Step Seven: Strengthening stepfamily ties

By now your family unit has had some happy and satisfying times together. As you have been getting to know each other better, you probably have been surprised at some of the things you have learned. Some may be happy surprises while others may seem annoying. There will certainly be ways in which people are very different from one another so that situations arise that are not comfortable for everyone. Talking together about differences and working out solutions to family problems can be challenging and rewarding. These family discussions can help by:
- Clarifying people's ideas.
- Clearing away misunderstandings.
- Seeing what the problem areas are.
- Giving people an opportunity to be active members of the family.

- Getting many suggestions for solving uncomfortable situations.
- Finding out places where family members agree.
- Deciding the best ways to deal with family challenges.
- Providing a time for people to plan together for their special family events.

A. Hold a family discussion once every two weeks

- Have a container in a convenient place and between meetings ask family members to put in slips of paper containing topics they wish to have discussed in the meeting. For example:

  Leslie didn't feed the dog on Thursday, and Blackie was hungry and whined all night. (Betsy)
  Where shall we go for our family vacation this August? (Dad/Eric)
  I hate it when Bill comes in my room without knocking. I want him to stay out. (Leslie)
  I'm feeling that we need to share the work here. It feels to me like I'm doing it all. (Mom/Betsy)
  Let's go to the rock concert in the park on Sunday. (Bill)

- Adults and children 12 and older take turns being in charge of the meeting. Younger children may need a little help with this, but it provides an opportunity for all family members to learn this type of skill and gain self-confidence.
- If there's not much to discuss, the meeting may be

short. It's important to get together regularly though, so that fun plans get discussed and annoyances don't go unnoticed and grow bigger because they don't get discussed.

- It can be a good idea to start with the topics that are easier to talk about or fun to plan. If all of the topics are difficult ones to resolve, you may need to talk a little about some of them and continue with more discussion at the next family meeting.

- "Brainstorm" and have a family member write down all the ideas without discussing if they will work or not.

- Go down the list and figure out which idea(s) will work the best, or combine ideas, or think of other ways that haven't been mentioned yet. Take Betsy's topic about the work around the house — the brainstorming might start like this:

   "Let's make a list of what needs to be done."
   "We can pick out what we want to do."
   "We could take turns cleaning."
   "Put up a list on the refrigerator and check it off."
   "Only clean every other week."
   "Let's sign up for what we want."
   "We could trade if we liked someone else's job better."
   "Let's hire someone."

   All of these (and any others) would then be discussed and a decision made.

- Decisions can be brought up again for further discussion and possible changes at future meetings.

- Schedule meetings when as many family members as possible are together. If children are left out, have a "mini-meeting" and fill them in. You may need different family solutions depending on who is in the household (e.g. Bill will feed the dog except on weekends when he's not there. Then Leslie will feed Blackie.)

- When people are upset, help them say how they are feeling without attacking another person. For example:

  "I'm mad at Bill. I need my room to be mine."
  (Not "Bill's terrible; he never does what I want.")

- If the discussion begins to be unproductive, you need to change the direction it's going by saying something like:

  "Let's talk about ways you think that could work out better."

  "What ideas do you have about how to do it differently?"

  "Both of you are feeling upset about this. Let's write a list of what would help."

  "Let's think some more about this and talk about it again next week — we're lucky, it can wait until then."

- Have a treat such as a chocolate sundae, a popsicle, or a special piece of fruit or cake at the end of the family discussion.

Family meetings can be difficult at times, but they can be extremely valuable for families. Sometimes it is hard to listen to others without wanting to defend yourself. If family members find that they can talk together in this way, the usual result is that angry or unhappy feelings get cleared away, and this lets the warm and happy emotions come out too. In this way, family members feel closer to one another.

Sometimes having productive family discussions starts out being too hard for families. It this is true for you, find a person you trust outside the household to lead the group until you are able to do it by yourselves. Families have sought this sort of assistance from the following kinds of people:

Friend	Minister
Therapist	School Counselor
Relative	Family Counselor

Learning how to talk together about things that bother you may take your family some time. We have tried to give you some suggestions about how to proceed, but it can be helpful to read more in detail about such meetings so they don't become unproductive "gripe sessions." Learning to talk together in this way with family members can make all your relationships smoother and can strengthen your family by increasing the respect and warm feelings all of you have towards one another. Do not rush the process. Move slowly in going on to the final step in this stepfamily integration program.

Step Eight: Working with the children's other household

When couples divorce, their children are losing contact with one or both parents. Since the children, except in very unusual situations, love both their parents, it helps them to have some ongoing contact with their two parents following the divorce. If your children have lost contact with their other parent, they may be wondering what's wrong with them that makes their other parent not want to see them. At times, this can be very upsetting to children, and it can make it more difficult for them to accept a new adult into their lives. The children need to hear it's not because of who they are.

At the same time that children may be wishing for contact with both of their parents, adults in stepfamilies may be finding it painful to have children move back and forth between households. Time tends to make this easier, and then the rewards of this position become evident:

- Parenting responsibilities are shared between more adults.
- There is a rest from some household responsibilities when the number in the household is less.
- Children gain an awareness that different households operate differently.
- Children have more adults to care about them. Being loved does not hurt!
- Adults can arrange to have the children cared for when they plan to be away.

One of the tensions for the adults in having the children coming and going between households, whether this happens frequently or infrequently, is the feeling of competition between households. You may fear that your children will want to stay longer in their other household. The adults in the other household may have the same fears regarding your household. As a result, it often happens that the children's two households grow more and more distrustful of each other. Then the children get caught in the middle and feel the adults' angry and hostile feelings going right through them like arrows.

Reducing these tensions between the adults in the two households can help children feel more comfortable and happy. Cooperation rather than competition also benefits the adults by producing the rewards just outlined.

If your children have contact with two households, Step Eight suggests one way to increase the cooperation between the adults involved.

A. Give the adults in the children's other household positive feedback once a month.

This can be a rewarding step to take because it can:
- Reduce feelings of competition between adults.
- Act as a model of behavior for the adults in your children's other household.
- Help your children relax so they relate more easily to you and your partner.
- Allow your children to feel better about themselves so they are easier for you to live with.

This positive feedback can be made in many ways:

By telephone	By parent or stepparent
In a note	In person
By the couple	

- Although your children usually would appreciate hearing you say something positive to them about their other household, do not ask them to relay the message.
- Give your positive comment or message without expecting a similar one in return. If you are basing your action on receiving the same in return, you could be disappointed and angry. If you are angry, your behavior will not help you or your children. Many times positive gestures are returned, but there is no guarantee!
- Positive comments usually refer to the children. Former (or present) difficult adult/adult relationships do not need to be resolved to give the following kinds of feedback:

    "We appreciated your making the effort to return Kelly early last week."

    "The kids had a wonderful time at the beach last Sunday."

    "We thought you might like to know that Suzanne had a fever this week but the doctor says she's OK now. She may be a little less energetic than usual though." (This comment indicates a thoughtfulness.)

    "Thanks for being there when we brought the children back."

    "Tom says you really did a good job helping him with his report on Africa."

- If you need to have a potentially tense discussion with the adults in the other household, do so when your children are not around. In this way they will not feel upset.

Unless the children are in their teens, make arrangements directly with the other adults. Saying to children, for example, "Tell your father he can pick you up at 6:00 on Friday" puts the children in the position of being messengers. Children usually resent this and often can unintentionally or intentionally get the messages mixed up.

- There are a number of other ways you can make it easier for your children to enjoy the benefits of having more than one parental household:

  Do not say negative things about the other adults in their lives.

  When they return, give children time to settle down in whatever way satisfies them before expecting them to relate to you.

  Let them know you want them to enjoy themselves in both households. (This can be hard to do, but it allows them to enjoy your household more fully also).

  Do not include the other household in disciplinary actions. If, for instance, one of your children is "grounded" for three days, but there are only two days left before he/she goes to the other household, the third day of grounding needs to occur when your child returns to your household.

We are not suggesting that you make the other adults good friends, although we know this can happen. We are suggesting that there are many advantages for you and your children in having a good business relationship between the adults who are involved with raising the children. Your former marital relationship no longer exists, so you will not be discussing personal issues; however, by respecting the parenting abilities of one another, a workable relationship may materialize between the two households.

If your former spouse is bitter and uncooperative, perhaps the feedback suggested in this Step will slowly make a difference. If it does not, it helps to remember that you cannot control the other household. You can, however, control what you do in your household. Everyone loses when members of households get into fighting with each other so unless it is an extremely important matter, you can simply choose not to fight. This ends the battle before it begins. Even when it's a struggle to see the children more, letting go can give you greater peace of mind in your household, and often results in your seeing your children more in the long run and having better relationships with them.

If you find that your family gets "stuck" and isn't able to grow as you would like, talking to a person who is trained to help stepfamilies work out their family relationships can be extremely valuable. Ask other stepfamilies who have met with someone about this if you have questions about how it can help. Stepfamilies have found help from resources such as the following:

Family Service
Jewish Family & Children's Services
Church counseling services
Therapists in private practice
Community mental health clinics
School counselors
Ask a counselor/therapist to contact Stepfamily Associa-

tion of American for information (address on page 90).

As a rule, families need to remain aware of the Steps and keep working on them. Even though you may not yet be satisfied that you have stepped ahead as far as your stepfamily can, your thought and effort to put these Steps into effect can make it possible for your family to experience many of the deep satisfactions that can come from living in this type of family. You will also become better at judging where to put your emotional energy for the greatest benefit. You will develop more realistic expectations so you will be disappointed less often. You can pat yourself on the back for taking these steps on the road to family unity, a family that is a comfortable and enriching place to live. The reactions of people who have participated in the Stepping Ahead Program speak for themselves:

> "More friends, more presents, more celebrations, more adults to love you, more children in the house to play with or do things with."
>
> "Awareness of what it takes to develop and maintain interpersonal relationships."
>
> "Never a dull moment."
>
> "A sense of personal growth."
>
> "More adult role models for me to choose from."
>
> "A stepparent who is more objective to confide in."
>
> "Another chance at happiness."

Conclusion

This Stepping Ahead Program can be used in a number of ways:

- By one stepfamily.
- By two or more stepfamilies who meet together to talk about the background material and their progress with the steps. (Perhaps you have friends or neighbors who would be interested).
- By a group who meets together with a leader on a regular basis.
- As a chapter program organized by a chapter of Stepfamily Association of America.

The following items may be ordered from Stepfamily Association of America:

- Stepfamilies Stepping Ahead books
- Leader's Manual
- Chapter Start-up Kit

To order any of these materials, please use the order blank at the end of this book.

With your order, you will be sent a list of pamphlets and books that may be ordered through our Educational Resources Program.

About STEPFAMILY ASSOCIATION OF AMERICA

Stepfamily Association of America, a national non-profit organization founded in 1979, is the only national association devoted to enriching stepfamily life through information, education, and support programs.

Your stepfamily is special with unique problems and needs. Our organization is dedicated to helping your family and all of society learn about what it's like to be part of a stepfamily. We want you to be able to work through the challenges, so you can enjoy the special rewards that only stepfamilies can experience. This book, Stepfamilies Stepping Ahead, is just one of the ways we provide help to stepfamilies. Some of our other programs include:

- Chapters around the country which offer special programs for stepfamilies including support groups. By getting together with other stepfamily members, you can learn how others deal with common stepfamily issues, gain support from other stepfamilies, and find solutions to the challenges you face.
- An Educational Resources program which makes available a wide selection of books about stepfamily relationships. Our Educational Resources catalog provides information about books that can be ordered and is available from our office. Send $4.00 for SAA's Educational Packet which contains this catalog, an issue of our quarterly publication *STEPFAMILIES*, legal information, and tips for stepfamily success.
- *STEPFAMILIES,* our quarterly publication containing timely information about issues stepfamilies find important and suggestions for professionals who work with stepfamilies (a sample copy is included in the above mentioned Educational Packet).
- An annual stepfamily conference with workshops and social events for stepfamily members and professionals.

Our association is supported by membership fees and contributions. Members receive a subscription to *STEPFAMILIES*, participation in the local chapter, a discount of 10% on any book orders, and reduced fees at our annual conference. You may use the order form at right, or contact the association office at the following address for more information or call us at (402) 477-7837:

STEPFAMILY ASSOCATION OF AMERICA
215 Centennial Mall South Suite 212
Lincoln, NE 68508

Although Stepfamily Association of America makes an effort to provide support and information throughout the United States, we know that there isn't always a chapter of Stepfamily Association in your area. Our Chapter Start-Up Program assists anyone in starting a chapter. The Start-Up Kit contains two manuals (Chapter Leaders and Learning to Step Together) and one booklet of helpful tips to get started. Or, if you just want to lead a support group, you may order the Support Group Leader's Manual and as many copies of Stepfamilies Stepping Ahead as you need.

To order either plus copies of Stepfamilies Stepping Ahead, please complete the form below. NOTE: All orders must be pre-paid. Please make checks or money orders to: Stepfamily Association of America, 215 Centennial Mall S., Suite 212, Lincoln, NE 68508 or use your credit card. Thank you.

Name _____ Address _____

City/State/Zip _____ Telephone # _____

Please Bill my ☐ MC ☐ Visa   # _____ Exp. date _____

Signature: _____

☐ YES, I want to purchase a Chapter Start-up Kit. Enclosed is a check for $25 plus $4.00 S & H.

☐ Please send me _____ copies of Stepfamilies Stepping Ahead. Enclose $9.95 for each copy plus postage at these rates: 1-4 copies: $3.00; 5-9 copies: $4.00, 10-16 copies: $5.00.

☐ Please send me _____ copies of the Support Group Leader's Manual. Enclose $9.95 for each copy plus postage at these rates: 1-4 copies: $3.00; 5-9 copies: $4.00, 10-16 copies: $5.00.

Stepfamily Association of America is supported by membership fees and contributions. We hope you will consider becoming a member, and making your contribution to the important work being done on behalf of stepfamilies. Basic membership dues (which are tax-deductible) are $35 per year. You'll receive a subscription to *STEPFAMILIES*, our quarterly publication, participation in your local chapter, 10% off any book orders, and reduced fees at our annual conference. Send in your membership application today and become part of a national organization which is making a difference in the lives of stepfamilies everywhere! Please consider one of the higher levels of membership. These are given special recognition in our conference program.

I would like to become a member of Stepfamily Association of America. Enclosed is my check for:

☐ $35   Individual/Family   ☐ $40-$90   Contributor
☐ $100   Donor   ☐ $250   Sponsor
☐ $500   Patron   ☐ $1,000   Benefactor

I do not want at this time to become a member of SAA, but I would like to subscribe to *STEPFAMILIES*, the quarterly newsletter of the Association. Enclosed is my check for:

☐ $14/year Individual/Family
☐ $16/year Foreign
☐ $22/year Agency/Organization

Name _____   Address _____

City/State/Zip _____   Telephone _____

Make check/money order payable to Stepfamily Association of America, 215 Centennial Mall South, Suite 212, Lincoln, NE 68508.